# The Barbarossa Brothers

## and the Pirates of the Mediterranean

### John Malam

QEB Publishing

Library of Congress Control Number: 2008010274

ISBN 978 1 59566 596 6

Printed and bound in the United States

Author John Malam (www.johnmalam.co.uk)
Consultant Philip Steele
Editor Amanda Askew
Designer Lisa Peacock
Picture Researcher Maria Joannou
Illustrators Peter Bull, Francis Phillips, Mike Saunders

Publisher Steve Evans

Creative Director Zeta Davies
Picture credits (t=top, b=bottom)
Alamy Images Mary Evans Picture Library 8, 9, 20
Art Archive Eileen Tweedy 14–15
Bridgeman Art Archive Collection of the New-York Historical Society 26, Private Collection/Archives Charmet 18, Private Collection/Peter Newark Pictures 17
Corbis Bettmann 27, Charles & Josette Lenars 25, Historical Picture Archive 27–28
Getty Images Hulton Archive 22, The Bridgeman Art Library 12
Mary Evans Picture Library Grosvenor Prints 13t
National Maritime Museum 21b
Rex Features Roger-Viollet 16
Topham Picturepoint The British Museum/HIP 13b

Words in **bold** can be found in the glossary on page 30.

# CONTENTS

# Pirate attack!

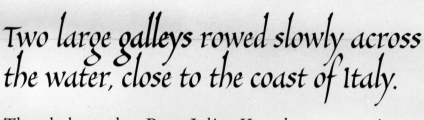

Two large galleys rowed slowly across the water, close to the coast of Italy.

They belonged to Pope Julius II and were carrying his goods. It was a journey that they had made many times before without mishap—but today was to be different.

It was 1504 and as the **papal** ships passed the Italian island of Elba, a small galley began to follow them. At first, the Pope's men on the first ship didn't think much of it, until they saw who was on board. When a lookout spotted that the strangers were wearing **turbans**, panic spread among the **crew**. The small galley was a **Muslim** pirate ship from north Africa, and it preyed on **Christian** ships.

The pirate captain, Aruj **Reis**, brought his galley alongside the larger ship. His men went on board and its crew were taken prisoner. Aruj and his men then disguised themselves in their captives' clothes —it tricked the second galley's crew, and they too were captured.

◀ *The galley of Aruj Reis closes in on the larger galley belonging to Pope Julius II. It was a daring attack.*

Aruj Reis took both **prize** ships to Goletta, his base in Tunisia, north Africa. For him, the greatest prize of all was the prisoners. The captured Christians became galley **slaves**, and they were forced to row the ships of their Muslim masters.

# Pirates of the Mediterranean: 1500–1650

## The Mediterranean Sea was the haunt of pirates long before Aruj Reis.

Pirates **plundered** ships and captured men, women, and children, who they sold as slaves or held hostage. The pirates' most famous hostage was Julius Caesar. He was captured in 75 BC and held for 38 days, until a **ransom** was paid for his release. Caesar returned to the pirates' den with help and executed them. The Mediterranean became a safer sea for travelers and merchants.

Spain

Italy

Mediterranean Sea

Morocco

Barbary Coast

Algiers

Tunis

⬆ *The Barbary Coast—a region along the coast of north Africa—was home to Muslim corsairs between about 1500 and 1650.*

Piracy returned to the Mediterranean in the AD 800s, when Muslim pirates from north Africa and eastern Spain began to raid Christian ships and towns. It was the start of a **holy war** that lasted for several hundred years. By about 1300, the worst of the fighting was over. Then, in the 1500s, Muslim pirates began to attack Christian ships and towns again, and a new period of Mediterranean piracy began. This was when the Barbarossa brothers— Aruj and Hizir Reis—were active.

## SHIVER ME TIMBERS!

Muslim pirates were usually given the title "reis" by their men. It is an Arabic word meaning "captain" or "commander."

6

# ROGUES' GALLERY

**Uluj Ali Reis**
*Active as a pirate*
*1550s–1587*

**Aruj Reis, "Barbarossa"**
*Active as a pirate*
*1500–1518*

**Hizir Reis, "Barbarossa"**
*Active as a pirate*
*1500–1544*

**Hamidou Reis**
*Active as a pirate*
*1790–1815*

**John Ward**
*Active as a pirate*
*1600–1623*

**Murat Reis**
*Active as a pirate*
*c.1565–1638*

# The Barbary Coast

For about 150 years from 1500 to 1650, the coast of north Africa was a safe haven for Muslim pirates.

Their realm stretched for hundreds of miles, eastward from modern-day Algeria to Libya. Although north Africa is now made up of countries, it was once a collection of **city-states** ruled by Muslim princes. The states were Tripoli, Tunis, Algiers, and Morocco. Europeans called the region the **Barbary Coast**, and the raiders who sailed out from its many ports were Barbary **corsairs**.

⬆ *A Christian priest buys back Christian slaves from their Muslim masters.*

## Corsair or privateer?

Corsair and privateer mean the same thing —raiders acting with the permission of their rulers. Corsair is for raiders from the north African or Barbary Coast, as well as France. Privateer is for raiders from Europe.

The Barbarossa brothers were amongst the first corsairs to sail from the ports of the Barbary Coast. As Muslim corsairs, they had permission from their city-states to raid non-Muslim targets—Christian towns and ships. As long as they did not break this basic rule and begin to attack their own people, Muslim corsairs believed that they were doing nothing wrong. Christians and other non-Muslims didn't see it this way at all. To their way of thinking, the Barbarossas, and men like them, were nothing more than pirates.

## SHIVER ME TIMBERS!

The word "Barbary" comes from "Berber," which was the name of the people who lived along the coast of north Africa.

⬇ If a captured Christian attempted to escape, the punishment was severe.

9

# A corsair galley

**Galleys were a common sight on the Mediterranean Sea, where they were used as merchant ships, warships, and pirate ships.**

All galleys were long, narrow **vessels** that sat low in the water. In the early 1500s, the galleys used by merchants to transport goods and people were up to 180 feet in length, while war galleys were about 150 feet in length.

Barbary corsairs preferred smaller galleys, known as **galiots**. They were about half the size of a merchant galley and were fast and easy to move around. Along each side of a galley was a row of oars. The oars were lined up in pairs, one on each side of the ship. On a corsair galley, each oar was pulled by two men. They were slaves or prisoners who were forced to work as rowers.

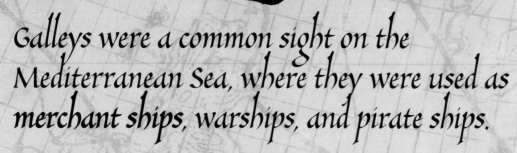

Main sail

Swivel gun

Deck gun

Ram

Anchor

It was their back-breaking effort that moved the galley through the water. At dash speed, a good crew could row one mile in six or seven minutes. They could keep this speed up for about 20 minutes, after which they would feel tired and the galley slowed down. It wasn't all hard work, though. On windy days, **sails** were used to move a galley along.

Captain's quarters

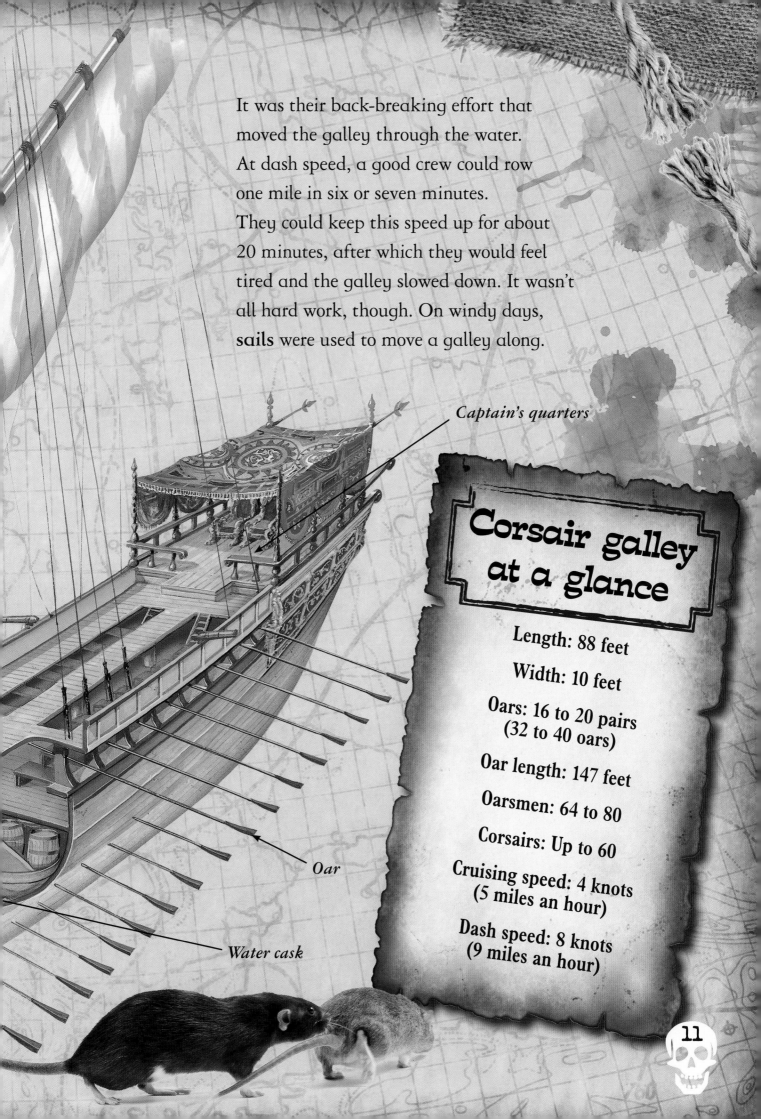

Oar

Water cask

## Corsair galley at a glance

Length: 88 feet

Width: 10 feet

Oars: 16 to 20 pairs
(32 to 40 oars)

Oar length: 147 feet

Oarsmen: 64 to 80

Corsairs: Up to 60

Cruising speed: 4 knots
(5 miles an hour)

Dash speed: 8 knots
(9 miles an hour)

# Galley slaves

**Taking prisoners was part of piracy in the Mediterranean Sea.**

Christian pirates took Muslims, and Muslim pirates took Christians, just as Aruj Reis did when he captured the Pope's galleys. Both sides turned their prisoners into slaves, and many were forced to work as "human machines" that rowed the galleys of their masters.

## SHIVER ME TIMBERS!

On June 20, 1631, the village of Baltimore, on the south coast of Ireland, was raided by Barbary pirates. More than 100 villagers were taken to north Africa and became slaves. In the 1600s, people were also snatched by corsairs from English towns in Devon and Cornwall.

◀ *Banks of Christian prisoners rowing a Muslim galley. The captain threatened them with harsh punishment if they stopped working.*

*Muslim corsairs making their getaway after attacking a vessel.*

Only men worked as galley slaves—women slaves were given other work, such as domestic work in their masters' houses. Galley slaves pushed and pulled at heavy oars for hour after hour. It was incredibly hard work. Some men worked as galley slaves for years, but many only lasted a short while. At sea, the slaves drank water mixed with oil and vinegar, and ate biscuits and **gruel**.

*Coins, pottery, and other objects have been found on a shipwreck near Morocco, north Africa. The ship might have been a corsair galley, on a raiding mission against English towns.*

There was a constant need for fresh and healthy galley slaves, and both Muslims and Christians went on raids to capture more men. By 1600, there were as many as 35,000 slaves in towns along the Barbary Coast. They were kept in overcrowded prisons called **bagnios**, some of which were owned by corsair captains.

# Attacked by corsairs

Corsair captains built up fleets of galleys. By 1512, Aruj Reis commanded 12 galleys and an army of several hundred men.

He would have needed at least 1,000 slaves to row his galleys, with many more held in reserve in the slave prisons of north Africa.

▶ *A corsair sword had a curved blade and is known as a scimitar.*

At first, Barbary corsairs only attacked vessels in the Mediterranean Sea, but by the 1600s, they were menacing ships and towns far away from their north African bases. Raids were carried out as far away as Britain, Ireland, and even Iceland.

A corsair galley had one small **cannon** at the very front. In an attack, the galley pointed toward its enemy, and when it was within range, the cannon was fired. By the time the gun was ready to fire again, the galley was too close to its enemy. At this point, the galley's soldiers climbed on board the enemy ship. They fought hand-to-hand, and when the fighting was over, the enemy ship and its crew had become the corsairs' prize.

⬇ *Corsair galleys in battle against larger sailing ships from Europe.*

## SHIVER ME TIMBERS!

In just seven years, between 1609 and 1616, Barbary corsairs captured 466 ships from around the coast of Britain, and thousands of men were taken prisoner.

# Aruj Reis:
## the one-armed corsair

Aruj Reis was the first in his family to embark on a life of piracy. He was a small man with a red beard and red hair.

His men called him "Baba Aruj," which meant "Father Aruj," but his Christian enemies called him "Barbarossa," which meant "Red Beard."

## Aruj Reis,
### known as "Barbarossa"

**Born:** 1470s, on the island of Lesbos, Greece

**Died:** 1518, at Oran, Algeria

**Occupation:** Corsair

◄ *Aruj Reis, together with his younger brother Hizir, were the most notorious of all the Barbary corsairs.*

In the late 1400s, Aruj attacked ships in the eastern Mediterranean. In one attack, he was captured by Christians and became one of their galley slaves. An Egyptian prince paid for Aruj to be set free, after which he settled on the Barbary Coast with his younger brother, Hizir. They made Tunisia their base, before moving west to a new base in Algeria.

Aruj raided Christian ships in the western Mediterranean. His most daring raid was in 1504, when he captured a pair of galleys owned by the Pope. The following year, he seized a Spanish warship with 500 soldiers. In 1512, during an attack on a Spanish fort in Algeria, Aruj lost his left arm. From then on, he wanted revenge against the Spanish, but in 1518, during a battle on the outskirts of Oran, he was killed by soldiers sent by the King of Spain.

# SHIVER ME TIMBERS!

In 1516, Aruj overthrew the ruler of Algiers and declared himself the new **sultan**, or prince.

◄ *Led by Aruj Reis, corsairs board the galley of Pope Julius II. The crew became his prisoners, and were taken to Tunisia, north Africa, where they began their new lives as galley slaves.*

# John Ward:
## the pirate who changed sides

Not all Barbary corsairs were born as Muslims. Some were Christian pirates who converted to Islam.

John Ward was an English pirate who began his pirate career raiding ships in the Caribbean. In about 1604, he fled to the Mediterranean, where he carried on plundering ships.

## SHIVER ME TIMBERS!

A traveler from Scotland visited Ward when he was an old man. He discovered that Ward had a hobby—raising chickens. He kept the eggs warm in camel dung!

◄ Pirates from the Barbary Coast capture slaves on the north Mediterranean coast.

# John Ward,
## known as "Yusuf Reis"

**Born:** c.1553

**Died:** 1623, of plague, in Tunis

**Occupation:** Pirate

It wasn't long before Ward came to the attention of Barbary corsairs, and by 1606 he had found a safe haven among them at Tunis. From there, he raided European ships carrying spices and gold. In one raid, Ward seized cargo worth $200,000, which he sold to Osman Bey, the ruler of Tunis, for $40,000. In return, Bey let Ward use his port. It was a small price to pay for his protection.

*Ward used his own money to buy freedom for English slaves held prisoner in north Africa.*

In 1610, Ward converted to Islam. He took the name Yusuf Reis, although many Muslims called him "Captain Wardiyya." He freed English slaves held in corsair prisons, and in England he was celebrated in songs. There was even a play written about him called *A Christian Turn'd Turk*. In the play, he was killed off at the end and his body was thrown into the sea. The real John Ward lived a life of luxury in Tunis and was waited on by English servants!

# Hizir Reis: the gift of God

Like his elder brother Aruj, Hizir Reis also had striking red hair and a red beard.

He was an educated man who spoke all the main Mediterranean languages— Greek, Arabic, Spanish, Italian, and Frenc

**↑** *Commanded by Hizir Reis, the Ottoman (Turkish) navy was the strongest force in the eastern Mediterranean, until losing the Battle of Lepanto in 1571.*

## SHIVER ME TIMBERS!

In 1529, Hizir used a fleet of 36 galleys to transport 70,000 Muslims from Spain to north Africa. It took seven trips to move them all.

After his brother's death in 1518, Hizir became the leader of the family's fleet of galleys. He continued the fight against Spain that his brother had begun. Hizir attacked Spain's possessions on the north African coast, and his galleys forced a Spanish fleet to retreat.

As Hizir grew in power, he was made ruler of the Barbary city-states, and in 1533 he was put in charge of the Ottoman (Turkish) navy. Two years later, he led a fleet of galleys to the Spanish island of Majorca. He looted the island and took 6,000 prisoners. In further raids, he attacked southern Italy and France, and defeated fleets of galleys sent by Spain, the Pope, and the cities of Italy.

The battle flag of Hizir Reis. The Arabic writing at the top says, "Mohammed! Reveal good news to the believers that the conquest is soon."

◀ In 1530, Hizir and his crew raided Tunis, capturing many slaves.

Hizir's success as a sea captain made the Ottoman navy the strongest force in the Mediterranean and he was given the title "Khayr-al-Din," which meant "the gift of God."

# Hizir Reis,
## known as "Barbarossa"

**Born:** c.1470s, on the island of Lesbos, Greece

**Died:** 1546, at Istanbul, Turkey

**Occupation:** Corsair and naval commander

# Murat Reis: Captain of the Sea

After being captured by a Barbary corsair when he was a teenager, he took the Muslim name "Murat."

Murat became a corsair captain, and as his attacks against Christian ships and towns increased, he gained a reputation as a powerful Muslim warrior. He was also very cunning.

↓ *Murat fought in the Battle of Lepanto in 1571. He was overpowered, along with the rest of the Ottoman navy by a stronger Christian force.*

## SHIVER ME TIMBERS!

Murat died while attacking the city of Vlore, Albania. He was probably about 100 years old at the time!

# Murat Reis

**Born:** c.1534, in Albania

**Died:** 1638, fighting in Albania

**Occupation:** Corsair and naval commander

When his ships attacked, he lowered the masts of his smaller galleys. Murat towed the little galleys behind his bigger ones, and because they were low in the water, they were hard to see. This tricked his enemy into thinking he had only a few ships and men.

▼ *Murat Reis approached a victim with care, sneaking up on a ship then mounting a sudden, surprise attack.*

Murat was the first Barbary corsair to venture out of the Mediterranean Sea. In 1586, he sailed through the Strait of Gibraltar—the narrow passage between Spain and north Africa —and into the Atlantic Ocean. He headed for the Canary Islands, off the coast of west Africa, and raided Lanzarote. Murat took the Spanish governor prisoner and only let him go after he was paid a large sum of money. In 1578, Murat was given the title "Captain of the Sea."

23

# Uluj Ali Reis: galley slave to sea captain

Thousands of Christian slaves rowed galleys for Muslim corsairs. Almost nothing is known about them, except for one. His name was Giovanni Dionigi.

He lived in southern Italy and probably expected to become a fisherman, like his father. However, in 1536, when he was about 16 years old, he was captured by a Muslim raider. It wasn't long before he was working as a rower on a Muslim galley.

It is believed that Giovanni Dionigi fell in love with his captor's daughter. In order to marry her, he converted to Islam and changed his name to Uluj Ali. From then on, he was a free man and decided to fight on the side of the corsairs.

← *Uluj Ali was a great leader and fought many battles, including the Battle of Lepanto in 1571.*

Uluj Ali became a leading corsair. He commanded a fleet of galleys, and led attacks against Spain and Italy. In 1571, he fought in the Battle of Lepanto, off the west coast of Greece. For five hours, about 300 Muslim galleys battled 200 Christian war galleys. Although the Muslim force was defeated, Uluj Ali fought bravely and led some ships to safety. After this, he became commander-in-chief of the Ottoman (Turkish) navy, and spent the rest of his life protecting the Barbary Coast from Christian attacks.

# Uluj Ali

**Born:** c.1520, in Italy

**Died:** 1587, in Istanbul, Turkey

**Occupation:** Corsair and naval commander

*The Battle of Lepanto lasted for about five hours. The Ottoman (Turkish) navy was defeated by a Christian force from Spain and Italy. It was the last major sea battle fought by galleys.*

# Captured crew

The golden age of Barbary corsairs ended around 1650—but this did not mean the Mediterranean was then safe for all ships.

The pirates of the Barbary city-states demanded **protection money** from ships, and in return they promised to leave merchant ships alone. In 1800, the ruler of Tripoli asked for more money, and the U.S. government decided to send a fleet of warships to fight the pirates. At first, all went well. The U.S. warships **blockaded** Tripoli, stopping pirates from entering and leaving the port.

◄ *The* Philadelphia *burning in the harbor at Tripoli, after the raid by Stephen Decatur.*

More warships were sent in 1803. One of them was the *Philadelphia*, but as it chased an enemy vessel, it became stuck close to the shores of Tripoli. The crew of 300 was taken prisoner. The pirates claimed the warship as their prize, and began changing it for their own use.

➡ *Lieutenant Stephen Decatur (in uniform, lying on the deck) fights the crew of a gunboat from Tripoli.*

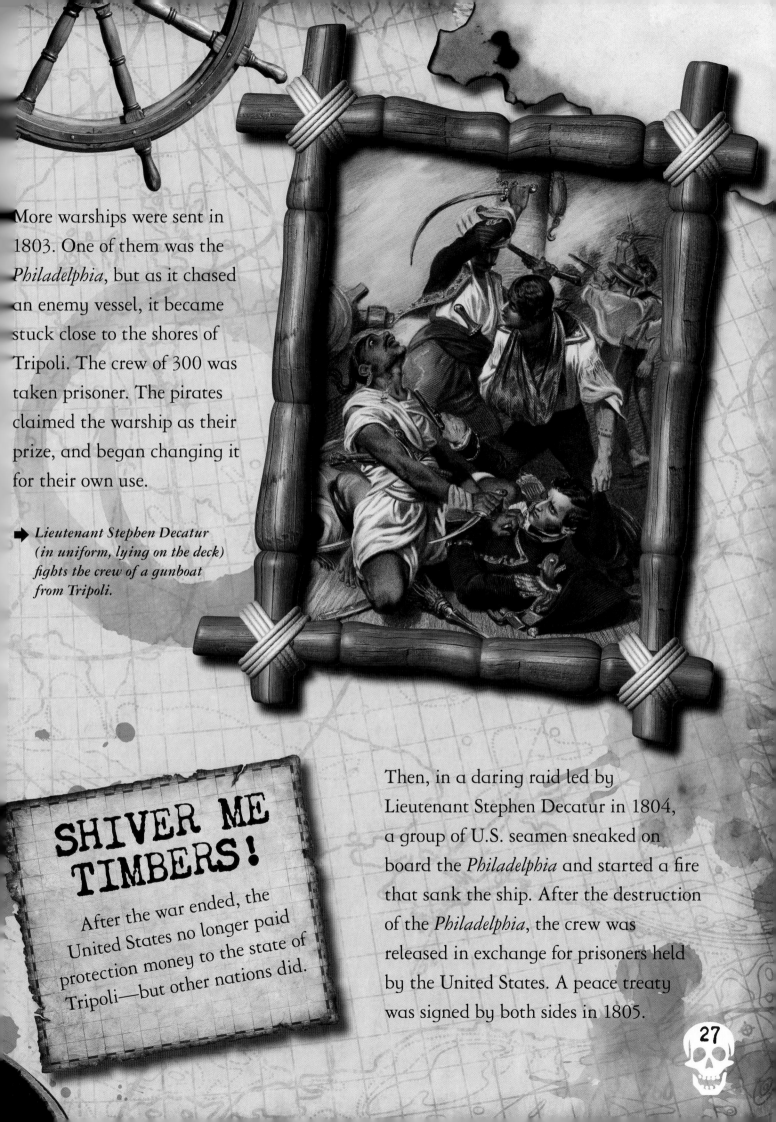

# SHIVER ME TIMBERS!

After the war ended, the United States no longer paid protection money to the state of Tripoli—but other nations did.

Then, in a daring raid led by Lieutenant Stephen Decatur in 1804, a group of U.S. seamen sneaked on board the *Philadelphia* and started a fire that sank the ship. After the destruction of the *Philadelphia*, the crew was released in exchange for prisoners held by the United States. A peace treaty was signed by both sides in 1805.

# Hamidou Reis: last of the corsairs

## The threat from Barbary corsairs finally ended in 1815.

A few years before, Hamidou Reis had made Algiers his base for raids against foreign ships. Between 1797 and 1800, he seized 19 ships and posed a serious problem in the western Mediterranean. Unlike his **ancestors**, Hamidou did not use galleys. Instead, he used ships with sails, and his flagship was armed with 44 cannon and carried a crew of 400 men.

### Hamidou Reis

**Born:** date not known, in Algeria

**Died:** 1815, off the coast of Spain

**Occupation:** Corsair

n battle, Hamidou showed
his cunning. In 1802, he raised
the British flag on his ship. As
he closed in on a Portuguese
vessel, they thought a friend was
approaching. It was a similar trick
to the one used by Aruj Reis 300
years earlier, when he disguised his
men in the clothes of his captives.
Hamidou took the Portuguese
ship, and went on to capture ships
from Denmark, Sweden, Holland,
Spain, Italy, Greece, and America.

⬆ *The death of Hamidou Reis, hit by
a cannonball and cut in two.*

*British and Dutch ships bombarded
Algiers, capital of Algeria, on
August 27, 1816. After the attack,
about 3,000 slaves were set free.*

In 1815, Hamidou was spotted off the coast
of Spain by a U.S. warship. The Americans
tricked him by using his own tactic of
flying the British flag, and the corsair let
them approach. In the battle that followed,
Hamidou was killed by a U.S. cannonball.

# GLOSSARY

**Ancestor**

A past member of someone's family.

**Bagnio**

A type of prison in north Africa where slaves were held prisoner.

**Barbary Coast**

An area of the north African coast, from modern-day Algeria to Libya, which was home to corsairs.

**Blockade**

To seal off a place, stopping people and goods from going in and out.

**Cannon**

A large gun on wheels that fired cannonballs and other types of shot.

**Christian**

Someone who believes in the ideas taught by Jesus Christ.

**City-state**

A self-governing city and its land.

**Corsair**

A pirate or privateer who operated in the Mediterranean Sea.

**Crew**

The people who worked on a ship. Also called the company.

**Galiot**

A small galley ship.

**Galley**

A type of ship powered through the water by oars.

**Gruel**

Boiled cereal, like porridge oats.

**Haven**

A safe place; a hideaway.

**Holy war**

A war fought between sides that have different religious beliefs.

**Islam**

The Muslim religion. The holy book is the Koran.

**Merchant ship**

A ship designed to transport goods.

**Muslim**

Someone who follows the religion of Islam.

**Papal**

Relating to the Pope.

**Peace treaty**

When opposite sides agree to be on friendly, peaceful terms.

## Plunder
To steal, or goods stolen by thieves.
Also called loot or booty.

## Privateer
A person who has permission from his
government or ruler to attack and steal
goods from his country's enemy.

## Prize
A ship taken as a reward.

## Protection money
Money given to someone in order to be
protected against attack.

## Ransom
Money that is paid to free someone who is
held as a prisoner.

## Reis
An Arabic word meaning captain
or commander.

## Sail
A large piece of strong cloth on the mast of
a ship, so the wind will push the boat along.

## Slave
A prisoner forced to do the work of
their master.

## Sultan
The ruler of a Muslim country or city-state.

## Turban
A man's headdress, made by wrapping a
strip of cloth around the head.

## Vessel
A ship or large boat.

# INDEX